SHE CHOSE *herself*

PINAL CHAUHAN

First Edition: September 2025
Printed in India

Printed at: Gapmeta Ventures Pvt. Ltd., Navi Mumbai
Typeset in Adobe Garamond Pro
ISBN: 978-93-6070-895-5

Cover Design: Prajakta Sawant

STORYMIRROR
Stories that reflect you

Publisher: StoryMirror Infotech Pvt. Ltd.
Unit No-F/705, 7th Floor, Kailas Corporate Lounge,
Veer Savarkar Road, Vikhroli Park Site,
Vikhroli West, Mumbai-400079,
Maharashtra, India.

Web: storymirror.com
Facebook: @storymirror
Twitter: @story_mirror
Instagram: @storymirror
Email: marketing@storymirror.com

Dedication

To every person who loved with their whole heart,
even when it was never fully held in return.

To the quiet warriors —
The ones who stayed soft in a world that asked them
to harden.

To the ones who broke, but rebuilt —
not louder, but wiser.

And to the one who never truly arrived,
Yet, it changed everything by showing up for a while.

She grew in the silence that followed.
And still — she loved anyway.

Author's Note

This is a work of fiction.

The characters — Anaya Malhotra and Aarav Nayak — are not real, but their emotions may echo something you've once carried:
a love that almost was,
a silence that hurt more than words,
and the slow return to oneself.

Though this story draws from life's quiet truths, it is not a memoir, nor an attempt to retell anyone's tale —
it is simply a journey of letting go, healing, and growing through love that didn't last... but still mattered.

This book would not have been possible without the silent strength and grounding presence of those who never left my side —

To Ganeshji—my quiet witness through every tear, every smile, and every late-night conversation I had with the universe.
To my parents, Bhadresh and Sumitra—who raised me with grace.
my siblings Shivali, Shaily, and Pratik—my constants through every storm.
my extended brothers Jasmin and Ingit- protectors in spirit.

My youngest heartbeat, Kian, whose laughter brings light;
Nirali—the one who stood between my breaking point and my becoming;
Vineeta—for being a steady ear and a warm space to lean on when I needed to talk and untangle my thoughts;
Unnati—for always holding a space for friendship in her own quiet way;
And lastly, all the beautiful people I hold dear but haven't named here.
Silky- my therapist and healer — thank you for helping me reclaim my voice.
Rangeela— whose presence shaped the pages and absence rewrote them.

If these pages find you at your most human —
May they also remind you: you are never truly alone.

— *Pinal Chauhan*

Prologue

She didn't know she was stepping into a love story —
not the kind with music and candlelight,
but the kind that shakes something loose inside you and
never gives it back the same.

This isn't her autobiography. But the words are from within.

It's the story of Anaya Malhotra — a woman who trusted again, long after she had forgotten how.
And it is the story of Aarav Nayak — the man who entered quietly, stayed just long enough to be unforgettable, and left behind a silence she had to grow through.

It's a story about believing too deeply.
And it is learning that sometimes, the greatest love doesn't stay —
But it still transforms everything.

It's fiction.
But everything in it looks so true.

Table of Contents

The Silence Before Him

Sometimes the loudest storms
are the ones no one hears.

The city around her was noisy — traffic, deadlines, expectations.
But inside her, silence screamed.

No one knew how much she'd buried to appear composed.
They called her strong, but didn't see that her strength had grown from broken roots.

There had been others —
A college predator who mistook control of the situation,
an ex-husband whose shadows were deeper than his existence.
He fractured her with kindness one day and fury the next.
She walked away with invisible bruises and a vow carved in steel:
Never again.

There were nights she didn't think she would make it.
nights when the ache was louder than logic,
and when even getting out of bed felt like betrayal to herself.
And in those moments,
It was Seher — her best friend, her lifeline —
who sat beside her in silence,
who picked up her shattered pieces without asking why they fell.

Seher never judged her brokenness.
She refused to let herself stay buried in it.

Years passed. She wore healing like armor, and independence like a badge.
But loneliness still lingered in the corners of her heart.

One night, over coffee and tired tears, Seher handed her a phone and said.

"What if there's someone out there who sees you...
and tries to fit into your life puzzle?
At least give it a shot."

She laughed.
She didn't believe it.
But that night, she downloaded the app anyway.

She didn't swipe out of hope.
She swiped out of defiance.
It was out of curiosity.
It was out of the quiet part of her that still wanted to believe.
Someone might find her beneath all the rubble.

The Stranger Who Felt Like Home

He wasn't trying to impress.
No filtered gym selfies, no pickup lines from borrowed movies.

Just one message:

"Swipe right only if you're interested in meeting. I am not here for endless chatting."

It was enough to pause her scrolling.

Their chats started slowly —
like tiptoeing barefoot after a heavy storm.
He asked about her dreams, not just her day.
He kept in constant touch.

His name was Aarav.

They never used the word love.
But there was a softness in how he asked if she'd eaten.
In the way he texted good morning before his meetings.
In how he made ordinary things feel gently extraordinary.

So she let her guard fall —
First, it was like a crack.
Then, it was like a door left open too long.

And just like that, it was...
A stranger felt like somewhere she'd been trying to get back to.

You brought a thousand shades into my grayscale world —
A little too Rangeela to stay,
and a little much for me to forget.

Plans & Promises

Some promises aren't broken.
They just dissolve in the distance.

He told her the news over a late-night video call.
His eyes sparkled — the way they did when he spoke about things that made him feel alive.

"They're transferring me abroad," he said.
"It's finally happening."

She smiled for him. Said all the right things.
She tried to hold her joy steady for him.
even as her heart quietly splintered behind the screen.

"Long distance is hard," he added,
"But I'll make it work. You matter."

She nodded, not wanting to ruin the moment.
She wanted to believe him.
Desperately.

But belief is a fragile house —
And distance is the storm that knocks on its door.
When love is still learning how to stand.

She watched him chase his dream across oceans.
And stayed behind with the promise that he'd return.
Some days, that promise warmed her.
Other days, it haunted the quiet corners of her waiting.

The Ghost of a Man Still Talking

It wasn't the silence that broke her.
It was the echo of someone who had already left,
still pretending to be there.

At first, he still replied — sporadically, softly, like a habit he wasn't ready to break.
He said he was busy. That time zones were hard. That he cared.
But his words had edges now, as if he were carefully stepping around something unnamed.

She asked about his days, his new world, and the distance between them.
He gave her crumbs of answers — always enough to keep hope flickering, never enough to feed it.

Then one day, it shifted.

Not with a breakup.
Not with an ending.
But with a sentence that lingered in her chest like smoke:

"Maybe we should just be friends."

She wanted to scream.
But instead, she opted to write.

Unsent Letter: "The Cracks"

Dear You,

You said it was distance that changed things.
But I wonder if it was just you...
You were pulling away before you ever fully showed up.

I knew when you lied. I felt it.

I saw it in the shift of your words.
The way you started hiding in the shadows of half-truths.
And yet — I stayed.
I kept loving you with open eyes.

Why did you think I couldn't handle the truth?

I was never looking for perfection.
Just honesty.

But I became an option
to someone I gave my all to.

Still, I didn't leave.
And maybe that's where I lost myself.

— Me

She couldn't hate him.
Even as he disappeared — one unspoken boundary at a time.
She grieved in quiet corners.
She talked less. Slept less.
Even her phone started feeling haunted —
lighting up only with memories.

And eventually, not even those.

So she began gathering her broken pieces.
One truth at a time.
One page at a time.
One poem closer to herself.

The Return

Not all returns come with a knock.
Some arrive as echoes in polite words.

She had begun to feel whole again —
not entirely healed,
but stitched back enough to breathe
without breaking.

Then one morning at 6:00 a.m.,
a message:

"Hi, thanks for the birthday wishes.
I missed responding earlier.
Hope you're well. Tc."

No emotion.
No acknowledgment of time lost.
Just a civil greeting
from someone who once held
her unspoken prayers.

It wasn't a conversation.
It wasn't even a connection.
Just a ripple in still water —
a presence making itself known
without depth.

And yet,
It stirred something.
Not hope.
Not longing.
Just a quiet ache.
for the version of her

who had once waited
for that very moment.

He hadn't returned.
He had simply resurfaced —
like a song you no longer loved,
but still remembered by heart.

She didn't respond.
Not this time.

Because sometimes,
your silence becomes
the only boundary left to draw.

And this time,
she wrote not for him,
but for the woman
who had survived
What he could never admit.

The Letters Never Sent

Some truths aren't meant to be delivered —
only released.

She never got to say everything.
Not when it mattered.
Not when it hurt the most.

So, she did the only thing she could do — she wrote.
Not for him to read. But for herself.
To honour what was real... even if it ended in silence.

Each letter was a timestamp —
One for when the world changed.
One for when it fell apart.

And though there were many more,
These were the two she returned to most —
Like bookmarks in a story she never quite finished.

Unsent Letter: "The Spark"

When We First Connected

Dear You,
I don't know if you'll ever read this — and maybe that's okay.

You came into my life like a calm I didn't know I was craving.
We didn't just talk — we connected.
Something about the way you spoke, the way you paused,
the way you looked at me like you already knew me from somewhere...
it felt like a soul meeting, not a moment.

I didn't fall for you instantly.

I grew into you.
And with every silent moment we shared, I saw something rare —
softness under your strength, depth under your detachment.

Did you ever feel it too? Even a little?

Because I still remember the warmth of that beginning.

– Me

♥ *Unsent Letter: "The Last Email"*

When It Ended

Dear You,
Your last message felt colder than any goodbye deserved to be.

There was no acknowledgment. No softness.
Just... finality wrapped in indifference.
And I read it — again and again —
hoping to find one crack where you still felt something.

I didn't want to change your mind.
I wanted to know I mattered.

But maybe that was always the problem —
I kept looking for worth in someone
who couldn't even be honest with me.

You hurt me.
Not just by leaving —

but by pretending I was never real.
And yet — I still wish you peace.
Maybe that's what love does when it's real.

– Me

She never hit send.
Because some goodbyes don't need answers.
Only release.

The rest of the letters?
They remained tucked away... waiting for the right pages to unfold.

The Book of Becoming

Some heartbreaks don't close the book.
They write a new one.

She stopped checking her phone.
Stopped wondering if he would unblock her, message her, apologize.

Something shifted.

Grief didn't vanish.
It grew quieter.
It sat beside her, instead of inside her.
She no longer felt like someone who had been abandoned —
she felt like someone becoming.

Healing wasn't loud.
It looked like coffee instead of tears.
Books instead of broken thoughts.
Small steps toward the version of herself she had buried for love.

And when she felt a familiar ache creeping in,
She didn't text.
She once again opted to write.

And Seher was still there,
never pushing her to move on faster,
Never judging the days that still hurt.
She didn't bring solutions —
She brought a presence.
Sometimes that meant late-night silences over coffee.
sometimes reminders to eat,
sometimes just sitting on the other end of a phone call,
breathing with her.

Seher didn't save her.
She simply didn't let her forget herself.

Unsent Letter: "The Healing"

Dear You,

You're not here anymore.
Not really.
Not in my messages.
Not in my plans.
Not in my future.

But sometimes I still feel your ghost —
The echo of what could have been.

I've stopped waiting for you to understand.
I've stopped needing your apology.

You may never know the full truth.
I saw every flaw in you — and still loved you gently.
I would've stayed, even through the storms —
if only you met me in honesty.

But now...
I'm writing this not for you — but for me.
To honour my own heart.

And to finally say:
I'm done carrying this alone.

— Me

This wasn't a story of losing someone.
It was the story of finding herself again.

In the stillness.
In the surrender.
In the soft voice inside her that whispered —

"You survived. And that is enough."

She didn't erase the past.
She wrote through it.

And what emerged...
wasn't just healing.
It was becoming.

I Loved You Anyway
She wrote her truth. She didn't wait for him to validate it.
She became her own closure.

And that — that was the real ending.

Unsent Letter: "The Mirror You Didn't Know You Were"

Dear You,

You didn't just walk into my life.
You arrived like a question I didn't know I was still asking.

You felt familiar, not because we were meant to last —
but because we were meant to collide.

They say when two souls share the same path numbers,
They recognize each other like old stars in a distant sky.
Maybe that's why it felt karmic, intense, inevitable.
Two Life Path Ones are orbiting our own ambitions.
They are mirroring the same fire — but with very
different fuels.

You, with your charm and ease,
I, with my scars and depth.
I mistook your presence for a promise,
your attention for devotion,
I mistook your silence for mystery — when it was really
just distance.

You held up a mirror I wasn't ready for
It was a mirror that didn't reflect us.
but it reflected me.

The girl who still believed despite everything.
The woman who wanted real love, not borrowed words.
The heart that gave — not because it was empty,
but because it was overflowing.

You weren'l capable of carrying my truth,
but you did carry my lesson.

And maybe that's why it still hurts.
Not because you broke me —
but because I offered you the version of me I waited years
to become
You didn't see her.

But I did.
And for that, I thank you.
I loved you anyway.

Hidden in Your Name

"Some loves don't spell out forever — they just remind you who you are."
"I see now that part of me lived inside your name, but you never learned how to pronounce me."

I used to trace the letters of your name in my mind, as if they held some hidden meaning.
I didn't realize until much later — they did.

Your name carried all the letters of mine, rearranged, almost scrambled — as if I were always meant to be a secret inside you. Not a chapter. Not even a sentence. Just a few soft vowels, sleeping between your syllables.

Maybe that's why I felt safe with you, even when you were emotionally unavailable. Maybe I mistook familiarity for fate.
I saw pieces of myself in you — and thought that meant we belonged.

But now I know:
It wasn't about being part of your story.
It was about recognizing mine —
even when someone else held the pen.

"I Was In Your Name"

Aarav Nayak: I was in your name
before I knew your story.
Tucked between the lines,
hidden in plain sight —
a soft constellation
spelled in silence.

ANAYA — five letters
waiting to be noticed
by someone who never looked close enough.
You spoke your name

like a shield,
not knowing you carried my syllables
like accidental luggage —
unopened, unnamed — "A. Nayak — which is Anaya"

Was it fate?
Or just some cruel poetry
that wrote me into your name
but never into your heart?

I thought
maybe you were meant to carry me —
just long enough
for me to remember
how it felt to belong.

But now I know:
I was only ever
a whisper inside you,
never a song you'd sing.

And yet —
I still loved you
for the echo.

Love doesn't always come to stay.
Sometimes, it visits with a mirror.
And if you're brave enough to look,
you'll find yourself — even in the people who couldn't hold you.

"I Saw You Before You Lied to Me"

"The hardest part isn't that you lied.
It's that I loved the version of you who didn't."

There was a version of you I met before the truth bent backwards.
Before the shadows crept behind your eyes and your words learned to dance around honesty.

That version was kind. Curious. Gentle in the way wounded people are when they don't want to hurt anyone else.
I saw him — not because you showed him to me,
but because I wanted to believe he was real.

The lie didn't break me.
It was the realization that you had no intention of being honest to begin with.
That you played sincerity like a song you didn't write.

And yet —
I still remember that first version.
The one that felt like the truth.
The one who didn't stay.

"The Time You Contacted Without Warning"

"Some moments don't change anything but they echo forever."

The time you contacted without warning,
I should have known I was still the soft place you turned to.
When no one else was available.
You weren't calling because you missed me.
You were calling because I still made you feel something.

I was calm — too calm, maybe.
As if my heart hadn't been waiting
to hear a version of your voice that might finally be honest.
But it wasn't.

You laughed lightly.
Like time hadn't stretched miles between us.
Like I hadn't cried in rooms you'd never walk into.
Like I hadn't rewritten my days without you in them.

You didn't ask how I'd been.
You didn't explain where you'd been.
You just picked up the thread as if it had never frayed.
And I —
I responded as if I hadn't been unraveling in your absence.

Now I know:
That call wasn't for me.
It was for your comfort.

And I answered it,
because I hadn't yet learned
that love isn't proven by whom returns —
but by whom chooses to stay.

"The Day I Stopped Hoping You'd Contact Again"

"Healing begins the moment you stop waiting for the apology."

There was no ceremony to it.
No thunder, no final message, no perfect closure.
It was just a quiet morning.
I reached for my phone.
And I realized I wasn't hoping to see your name.

It startled me.
how natural it felt .
to not ache.

I used to read silence like a language,
decoding every hour you didn't text
as proof that I still mattered somehow.
That maybe you were thinking of me.
Maybe your pride was just in the way.
Maybe.

But that day,
I didn't search your silence for signs.
I didn't imagine your excuses.
I didn't beg the universe for a sign.

Because the truth had been speaking all along.
You just never planned to stay.
And I finally stopped pretending you would.

There was no anger.
There was only a gentle kind of grieving.
It was for the version of me who waited far too long.
It was for someone who never looked back.

"I Never Blocked You"

"Leaving the door open wasn't a mistake.
It was love — honest, flawed, and mine."

I never blocked you.
It was not because I couldn't.
But it was because some part of me still believed.
You might return —
This time without the lies,
Without the mask,
Without the mess.

There was no ego in it.
Just the hope that maybe,
if you ever grew tired of pretending,
you'd remember where truth felt safest.

With me.

People say you should cut the cord.
Delete, block, disappear.
But I wasn't ready to erase the only place
where my love had ever reached you —
even if it was only one-way.

Some nights I imagined it:
Your thumb hovering over my name,
heart pounding,
ready to tell me everything you never said.

You never did.

And I never blocked you.
Not because I was waiting —
but because I wanted to be someone who didn't have to
shut the door to survive.

"If You Ever Come Back"

If you ever come back,
You'll find no anger here.
No speech rehearsed.
No storm waiting at the threshold.

Just a quieter version of me —
The one who learned how to stay
without losing herself.

I loved you
without punishment.
Without revenge.
Without erasing you.

That, I think,
was the loudest goodbye of all.

"Blocked"

"Some endings aren't endings,
they're escapes from a truth too heavy to face."

One day, without warning,
you were just... gone.
Blocked. Erased.
It was not after a fight. It was not after closure.
Just vanished from my screen
It was like I had imagined everything.

But what hurt wasn't the block.
It was the way you stayed so comfortably in my life
before it.

As if nothing had happened.
As if you hadn't disappeared on me once.
As if cozy conversations could cover up
all the confusion you left behind.

You spoke to me like we hadn't cracked.
Like I hadn't waited, wondered, forgiven,
more times than I should've.

And still, behind those smiles,
you were already with someone else.
You were chatting with someone new.
You were slipping into the same patterns
with different people,
while making me feel like I was the only one still holding on.

I asked for one thing.
A last meeting. A real goodbye.
You said you were away —
but I knew better.

I gave you time.
I hoped you'd choose presence over pretense.
You didn't.

And when the weight of all your silences finally fell
you blocked me.

As if I had wronged you.
As if I hadn't held your secrets,
your softness,
your contradictions
with care.

You didn't need to explain.
You just needed me gone
so the mirror I had become
would stop showing you your own reflection.

I wasn't angry that you blocked me.
I was just heartbroken
that I meant so little to someone
I had loved so much.

"Midnight, A Month Too Late"

"Some apologies don't come late — they never come at all.
Only accusations arrive, dressed as defense."

After everything, I sent him one last message.
No anger. No blame.
Just one door, left slightly open —
a moment for peace, if he wanted it.

He didn't respond.

Not when it mattered.
Not when I was still in the city.
Not when he could've shown up and spoken his side.

But nearly two weeks later,
At midnight,
came a reply.

Not a memory.
Not a feeling.
Just a complaint.

I had offered him closure.
He offered me a threat.

It wasn't the content that hurt.
It was the timing.
The coldness.
The ease with which he bypassed all the ways he had
confused, lied to, and used me —
and the turning of the spotlight on the one moment I
cracked.

As if that one crack made me the villain.
As if his countless masks didn't weigh more.

I didn't reply.
Not because I was guilty —
but because I finally understood the truth:

Some people don't want peace.
They want control over the narrative.

If He Ever Comes Back

"You don't burn bridges when you're still standing on the ash,
but you don't rebuild them alone, either."

There's no hatred left.
Just silence — the kind that comes
when your soul finally stops screaming.

He never really said goodbye.
Not when he vanished.
Not when he blocked me.
Not even when I offered him...
One last chance to show up with grace.

And when he finally replied,
It wasn't regret.
It was an accusation —
efficient, pointed, and cold.

He said I had wronged him.
without ever asking himself how his own actions had hurt me.
He never paused to see the gap between what he said and what he did.
the intimacy he extended while being with someone else,
the lies about where he was,
the silence when truth was all I asked for.

People had warned me about him long before.
He had already been exposed by someone else.
But I never felt the need to add to that noise.
I didn't need to tear him down.
I chose to follow my heart.
to believe in the man I thought he could be,
to stand by him because I trusted him.
Even when he made it hard.
And perhaps, deep down,
I still do.

So if one day...
he looks at everything.
with clearer eyes...
If the weight of his choices finally lands...
If truth starts whispering louder than pride —

Then maybe, he'll reach out.
He knows how.

He always knew how.

And if he does,
I won't be waiting.
But I won't be angry either.

I'll be living.
Lighter.
Wiser.
Somewhere between forgiveness and forgetfulness.

And if he ever stands in front of me again,
not to defend himself but to understand me —
then maybe,
just maybe,
there might still be
a story left to write.

But this time,
he'll have to earn every word.

"Things I Chose Instead"

She stopped waiting to be chosen.
And quietly, powerfully — chose herself instead.

I chose
morning coffee
over morning tears.

Long walks with no destination,
instead of walking in circles of what-ifs.

Trekking uphill with old friends,
instead of dragging dead conversations downhill.

A mat and a mirror in Pilates class,
to face the woman I was becoming —
not the one he broke.

I chose
ink over anxiety.
Pages over pleading.
Poems over patterns
I no longer wanted to repeat.

I chose
sitting at the dinner table,
really listening —
not checking for messages that never came.

I chose
truth in movement.
Grace in silence.
A job to chase,
not a ghost.

I didn't heal overnight.
I simply began
choosing again,
and again,
and again —
until my life no longer resembled the ache
I once mistook it for love.

The Lightness I Almost Forgot

It didn't happen all at once —
but one day, she exhaled
and realized she felt light again.

I forgot
what it felt like
to laugh with my head thrown back
and mean it.

To dance in my room with the music too loud
and the curtains too open —
without wondering
who might be watching,
or judging, or leaving.

I forgot
that healing doesn't always whisper.
sometimes, it roars.

In passport stamps.
In Pilates sweat.
In new lipstick shades
I wear just for me.

I forgot how
freedom feels
saying "no,"
and not explaining.

How joy doesn't knock —
it walks in
When you stop waiting at closed doors.

The lightness came back slowly.
Not in grand gestures.
But in small things.

Waking up without checking my phone.
Letting a day pass without naming him.
Smiling at my own reflection.
Breathing like I belong
to no one but myself.

This isn't revenge.
This isn't recovery.

This is what it looks like.
When a woman returns to herself —
unapologetically,
deliberately,
wholly.

Because you don't need
a new name in your phone,
or a warm body next to yours,
to feel alive again.

Sometimes,
moving on
just means
coming home to yourself.

If I Ever Believe Again

"Some things break you open just so you can grow into someone softer."

She never thought she'd stop checking the unread messages folder.
Never thought she'd stop writing replies in her head to a man who never truly listened.

But healing isn't loud.
It doesn't come with fanfare or final words.
It comes in a quiet morning where she doesn't think of him first.
In a coffee cup that doesn't remind her of old conversations.
In a laugh that feels like hers again.

And one day, when someone says "You have kind eyes,"
She won't flinch.

She'll smile — not because she's ready to love again,
but because for the first time in a long time...
She's not afraid of it.

That's what grace does.
It doesn't erase the story.
It softens its sharpest parts.

And so she wrote —
not to send,
but to finally let go.

Unsent Letter – "Letting Go with Grace"

Dear You,

I don't hate you.
I don't wish you pain.

I wish you the kind of love I offered —
the kind that doesn't leave when it gets hard.

Maybe someday you'll come across this.
Maybe you won't.
But just in case you do — know this:

I never had ill intentions.
I never played a game.
I just... loved you. Purely. Quietly. Fully.

And now I'm choosing to let go —
not because I stopped loving you...
but because I finally started loving myself more.

Goodbye, not with bitterness.
But with light.

– Always, Me

"A Letter to the Woman I'm Becoming"

She didn't rise from the ashes.
She learned to stop setting herself on fire.

Dear You,

You held on longer than you should have.
Not because you were weak,
but because you loved that deeply.

You kept giving chances
even when it cost you sleep, self-respect,
and sometimes your voice.

You thought love meant holding on.
But now,
you know that love sometimes means letting go —
of people,
of guilt,
of versions of yourself
that only existed to please someone else.

You're not bitter.
You're just done explaining yourself to people
who only ever saw the surface
and not the storms you survived.

You've learned to ask different questions now.
Not:
"Will he stay?"
But:
"Do I feel safe here?"
"Can I breathe?"
"Do I still recognize myself?"

That's growth.
That's grace.

And in case no one told you today:
I'm proud of you.

Not because you've figured it all out,
but because you've stopped pretending you need to.

With love,
The version of you who never gave up.

"I Know This Now"

She no longer waits to be chosen.
She chooses herself — every time.

I don't know what tomorrow holds.
But I know who I am today.

I know what I gave,
and I know what I'll never settle for again.

I know love isn't meant to confuse,
to hide,
to manipulate,
or to only show up when it's convenient.

I know that silence can be cruel,
but self-respect is louder.

I know I can rebuild myself —
not from someone's approval,
but from my own truth.

I know I have scars.
But I also have softness.
And the strength to carry both with grace.

I know I'll still believe in connection —
But this time.
it'll be mutual.
It'll be steady.
It'll feel like home — not a hurricane.

And most of all —
I know this isn't the end of my story.
It's just where I stopped looking for love
in the wrong places.

"For Anyone Who Needs to Hear This"

You weren't too much.
They just weren't ready for someone real.

You are not foolish for loving.
You are not weak for hoping.
You are not broken because someone couldn't see
your worth.

Sometimes, we give the best of ourselves
to people who are still searching for their own peace.
That doesn't make you wrong — it makes you human.

If your heart was used,
If your trust was tested,
If your silence held more weight than their words ever did

This is your reminder:
You still win,
You loved with honesty.

But healing...
Healing is the real victory.
The real victory is not revenge.
Not explanations.
Just the quiet act of choosing yourself,
again and again,
until it no longer hurts to do so.

And if you're lucky,
you'll have one person beside you —
the kind who doesn't fix you,
but reminds you you're not too broken to begin again.
The kind of person who stays,
even when you push the world away.
Someone like Seher.

You don't need a new person to move on.
You don't need closure from someone who never cared to offer it.
You just need to come home — to you.

You are allowed to begin again.
With better boundaries.
With softer eyes.
With a stronger heart that now knows
what it will and will not allow.

If you're reading this and your story feels like mine,
I hope you choose peace over proving your worth.
I hope you protect your energy.
but keep your soul open to joy.

And above all.
I hope you remember this:

Not everyone left.
Some love stayed — and helped you rise.